LabSim®

The Lessons Only Experience Can Teach

Security+

Custom Publishing

New York   Boston   San Francisco
London   Toronto   Sydney   Tokyo   Singapore   Madrid
Mexico City   Munich   Paris   Cape Town   Hong Kong   Montreal

Pearson
Custom Publishing
is a division of

www.pearsonhighered.com

ISBN 10: 0-555-05125-0
ISBN 13: 978-0-555-05125-2

Contents

0.0 Introduction... 1

   0.3.2 Create a Local User Account 2

   0.3.3 Change the Account Type 4

   0.3.7 Create a Domain User Account 5

   0.3.8 Disable a User Account 8

   0.3.9 Reset the Password.. 10

   0.4.3 Create a User 11

2.0 Cryptography.. 15

   2.3.3 Enforce Password Settings.. 16

   2.3.4 Configure Account Lockout... 19

   2.3.5 Disable Last Logon Name 21

   2.3.7 Modify Password Properties 22

   2.3.8 Restrict Logon Hours 25

4.0 Authentication 27

   4.1.5 Enforce NTLM Authentication.. 28

5.0 Network Infrastructure Security 31

   5.2.2 Share an Internet Connection 32

   5.2.4 Configure NAT 35

   5.3.5 Enable ICF.. 38

5.3.6 Open ICF Ports.. 39

5.3.7 Close Open Ports... 42

5.3.8 Prevent ICMP Events 43

5.4.2 Create a Packet Filter 1.. 45

5.4.3 Create a Packet Filter 2.. 47

5.4.5 Apply Access Lists to Interfaces 49

5.4.6 Restrict Traffic from Specific Hosts.................................... 51

5.4.7 Restrict Traffic from Specific Networks 53

5.5.2 Create a VLAN and Assign Ports...................................... 55

5.5.3 Exploring VLAN Communication 56

6.0 Network and Application Hardening.. 59

6.2.4 Disable File and Printer Sharing... 60

6.2.5 Uninstall a Component 62

6.2.6 Disable NetBIOS over TCP/IP 64

6.2.9 Enforce SMB Signing... 66

6.3.7 Stop and Disable Services 68

6.4.2 Format a Drive.. 70

6.4.3 Convert a Drive... 72

6.4.5 Change NTFS Permissions... 73

6.4.6 Configure NTFS Permissions... 77

6.4.8 Encrypt a File 79

6.4.9 Encrypt a Folder and Contents... 81

6.5.2 Modify File System Rights.. 82

6.5.3 Add a Trustee and Rights 84

6.5.5 Modify Folder Attributes.. 87

7.0 Auditing and Intrusion Detection.. 89

7.1.4 Enable Auditing 1 90

7.1.5 Enable Auditing 2 92

7.1.7 Save the Audit Log... 94

7.1.8 Change Log Properties 95

7.1.9 Configure the System to Shut Down... 97

8.0 Communication Security **99**

8.1.4 Configure a Remote Access Server 100

8.1.6 Create a Remote Access Policy.. 102

8.1.8 Create a Dialup Connection 106

8.1.9 Configure Advanced Authentication... 109

8.1.10 Configure Smart Card for Authentication 111

8.2.4 Configure a VPN Server.. 112

8.2.5 Disable PPTP Ports.. 114

8.2.7 Create a Client VPN Connection 117

8.2.8 Customize the Tunneling Protocol 118

9.0 Internet Services Security **121**

9.1.4 Configure Web Site Authentication.. 122

9.1.5 Configure Web Folder Authentication 125

9.1.7 Configure IIS Permissions.. 126

9.4.2 Clear the Browser Cache 128

9.4.4 Add a Trusted Site.. 130

9.4.5 Add a Restricted Site.. 133

9.4.6 Customize Zone Settings.. 136

9.4.8 Change the Cookie Level.. 138

9.4.9 Customize Cookie Handling... 140

9.4.11 Configure Browser Security 142

9.4.12 Clear Temporary Internet Files.. 144

0.0

Introduction

0.3.2 CREATE A LOCAL USER ACCOUNT

Scenario

You have just purchased a new computer for use at home. You want to provide some measure of security and limit the types of actions your children can do while logged on to the computer.

Complete the following tasks:

- Create a new user account named *kids*

- Make the account a limited user account

- Set the password to *jump*

- Configure the password hint to read: *what you do with a rope*

Steps

Complete the following steps:

1. Click **Start/Control Panel**.

2. Click **User Accounts**.

3. Select the **Create a new account** task.

4. Type a name for the new account. Then click **Next**. (The user name and full name will be set to the name you type.)

5. Select the account type for the new user account.

Which account type would you choose to create a user capable of doing the following tasks?

Task	Account Type
Access files created by the user	
Change the user password and picture	
Create and modify user accounts	
Install programs	
View files in the Shared Documents folder	

6. Click **Create Account.**

7. Click the account you have just created.

8. Click **Create a password.**

9. Type the new password (twice) and the password hint. Click **Create Password.**

0.3.3 CHANGE THE ACCOUNT TYPE

Scenario

You have just installed Windows XP on a home computer and created a few user accounts. Your sister, Mary, is using the computer as well. She tells you, however, that she is unable to install some of her favorite programs.

Give Mary additional privileges on the computer by changing the account type. Make the account a computer administrator account.

Steps

Complete the following steps:

1.   Click **Start/Control Panel**.

2.   Click **User Accounts**.

3.   Select the account you want to modify.

4.   Click **Change the account type**.

5.   Select the account type (either **Computer administrator** or **Limited** use account). Click **Change Account Type**.

0.3.7 CREATE A DOMAIN USER ACCOUNT

Scenario

You are a network administrator for your company. Your company has a single Active Directory domain named westsim.private. You are responsible for creating and maintaining user accounts in the domain.

A new employee named U Smith has joined your company as a Sales employee.

Your task in this lab is to create a new domain user account for the new employee with the following values:

- User account context = Sales OU

- First Name = Sally

- Initials = [None]

- Last Name = Smith

- Full Name = Sally Smith

- Logon Name = ssmith

- UPN Suffix = westsim.private

- Pre-Windows 2000 Logon Name = ssmith

- Password = sallysmith

- User must change password at next logon = Enabled (keep all other account options disabled).

Steps

In this lab, use Active Directory Users and Computers to create a user account.

Complete the following steps:

1.   Click **Start/Administrative Tools/Active Directory Users and Computers.**

2.   Right-click the Sales OU and select **New | User.** The following dialog is shown.

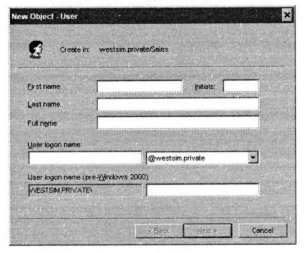

3. Enter the values for the account you want to create. Click **Next**. The following dialog is shown.

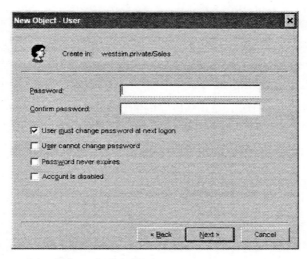

4. Type the password (twice) and click **Next**.

5. Click **Finish**.

0.3.8 DISABLE A USER ACCOUNT

Scenario

You are a network administrator for your company. Your company has a single Active Directory domain named westsim.private. You are responsible for maintaining user accounts in the domain.

A user in the Accounting department named Addie Henfield is leaving for maternity leave. You want to prevent her user account from being used while she is gone.

Your task in this lab is to disable the Addie Henfield user account.

Steps

Complete the following steps:

1. Click **Start/Administrative Tools/Active Directory Users and Computers**.

2. Click the **Accounting** OU. A list of objects in the OU are shown on the right.

3. Right-click the **Addie Henfield** account and select **Disable Account** from the menu.

4. Click **OK**.

   What has happened to the user account icon?

   _____

5. To view the user account setting that disables an account, right-click the account and choose **Properties**.

6. Click the Account tab. The following dialog is shown.

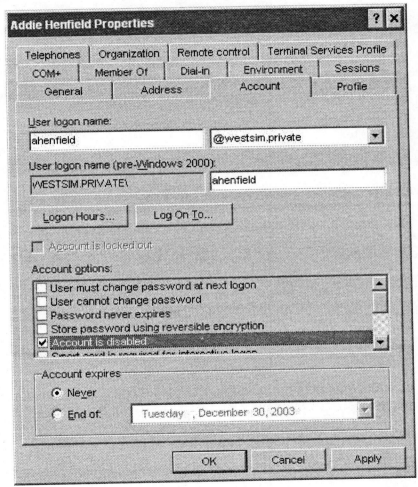

Note the **Account is disabled** option.

7. Click **Cancel** to close the dialog.

0.3.9 RESET THE PASSWORD

Scenario

You are a network administrator for your company. Your company has a single Active Directory domain named westsim.private. You are responsible for maintaining user accounts in the domain. Samantha Holden in the Shipping department has forgotten her password.

Your task in this lab is to:

- Reset the password for the Samantha Holden user account to samantha.

- Require her to change her password at next logon.

Steps

Complete the following steps:

1. Click **Start/Administrative Tools/Active Directory Users and Computers**.

2. Click the **Shipping** OU. A list of objects in the OU are shown on the right.

3. Right-click the **Samantha Holden** account and select **Reset Password…**.

4. Type the new password (twice) and select **User must change password at next logon**.

   If a user is currently logged on, what must the user do before the new password will take effect?

   _____

   Click **OK**.

5. Click **OK**.

0.4.3 CREATE A USER

Scenario

Rajeev Agarkar was hired into the IS department in Seattle. Create the RAgarkar.IS.Seattle. WestSim user object. Assign the following properties:

- Password = go4IT!

- Full Name = Rajeev Agarkar

- Title = Technician

- Telephone = (206) 360-5641

Steps

User accounts in eDirectory are created using ConsoleOne. When the lab starts, ConsoleOne is already open.

Complete the following steps:

1. Start by browsing to the parent container that will hold the user object. Expand the **WestSim-tree** object, followed by the **WestSim** organization object, followed by the **Seattle** organizational unit.

2. Right-click the **IS** container and select **New | User...** from the menu. The following dialog is shown.

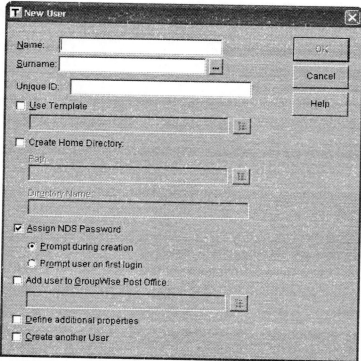

3. Enter **RAgarkar** for the name and **Agarkar** for the surname. Click **OK**.

4. Type the password (twice), then click **Set Password**.

5. Right-click the new user account icon in the right window and select **Properties...**. The following dialog is shown.

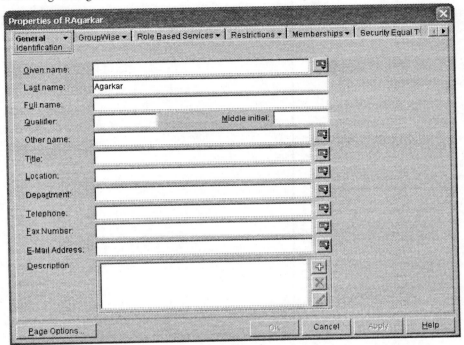

6. Fill in the **Given name**, Full name, **Title**, and **Telephone** properties. Click **OK**.

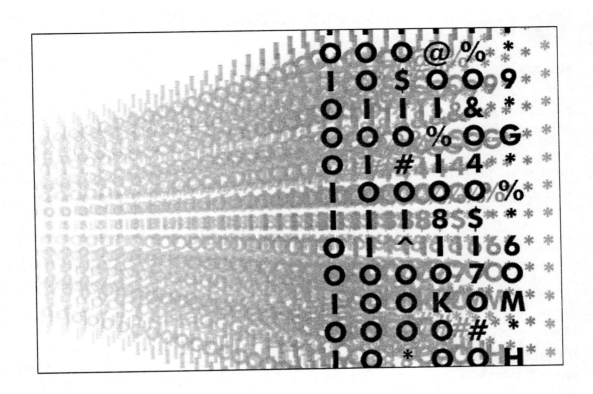

2.0

Cryptography

2.3.3 ENFORCE PASSWORD SETTINGS

Scenario

You are a network administrator for your company. Your company has a single Active Directory domain named westsim.private. You want to increase the complexity of passwords used on all computers throughout the network.

Your task in this lab is to configure the domain's password policy to meet the following requirements. Passwords must:

- Be at least 8 characters

- Contain uppercase letter, lowercase letter, number, and symbol characters

- Be kept for at least 14 days

- Be changed at least every 90 days

- Be different than any of the user's previous 24 passwords.

Steps

In this lab, you need to edit the Default Domain Policy (linked to the domain object). In the GPO, browse to **Computer Configuration/Windows Settings/Security Settings/Account Policies/ Password Policy** and edit the various password policy settings.

Before beginning, complete the following table with the necessary values:

Policy	Setting
Enforce password history (the number of unique old passwords to track)	
Maximum password age (the maximum time a password can be used)	
Minimum password age (the minimum time a password can be used)	
Minimum password length	
Passwords must meet complexity requirements (whether password must contain additional character types)	

Complete the following steps:

1.   Click **Start/Administrative Tools/Active Directory Users and Computers**.

2.   Right-click the domain and select **Properties**.

3.   Click the **Group Policy** tab. The following dialog is shown.

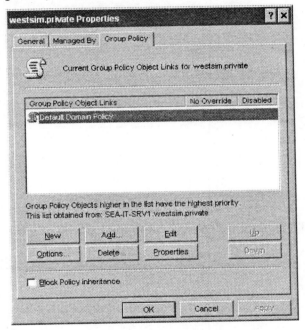

4.   Select the **Default Domain Policy** GPO in the list, then click **Edit**.

5.   Browse to **Computer Configuration/Windows Settings/Security Settings/Account Policies/Password Policy**.

6.   For each policy you need to edit, right-click the policy and select **Properties**. A dialog similar to the following is shown.

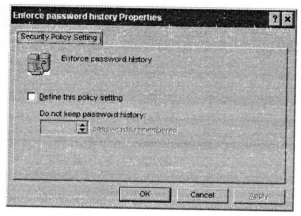

7.   Click **Define this policy setting**. Configure the appropriate value, then click **OK**. (Click **OK** as necessary to accept suggested value changes.)

8.   Repeat steps 6 and 7 for every policy you need to define.

9.   Close the Group Policy editor.

10.   Click **OK** to close the domain properties.

2.3.4 CONFIGURE ACCOUNT LOCKOUT

Scenario

You are a network administrator for your company. Your company has a single Active Directory domain named westsim.private. You are concerned about unauthorized users trying to break into the domain. As part of securing the domain, you decide to create an account lockout policy.

Your task in this lab is to configure the domain's account lockout policy to:

- Lock out any user who enters three incorrect passwords within a 30 minute interval.

- Keep the user account locked until you (or another administrator) unlock the account.

Steps

In this lab, you need to edit the Default Domain Policy (linked to the domain object). In the GPO, browse to **Computer Configuration/Windows Settings/Security Settings/Account Policies/ Account Lockout Policy** and edit the various settings.

Before beginning, complete the following table with the necessary values:

Policy	Setting
Account lockout duration (how long the account is locked out)	
Account lockout threshold (the number of wrong passwords allowed before account lockout)	
Reset account lockout counter after (the time period in which the number of wrong passwords is tracked)	

Complete the following steps:

1. Click **Start/Administrative Tools/Active Directory Users and Computers**.

2. Right-click the domain and select **Properties**.

3. Click the **Group Policy** tab.

4. Select the **Default Domain Policy** GPO in the list, then click **Edit**.

5. Browse to **Computer Configuration/Windows Settings/Security Settings/Account Policies/Account Lockout Policy**.

6. For each policy you need to edit, right-click the policy and select **Properties**.

7. Click **Define this policy setting**. Configure the appropriate value, then click **OK**. (Click OK as necessary to accept suggested value changes.)

    Tip: When setting the **Account lockout duration**, set the value to 0 and read the text description.

8. Repeat steps 6 and 7 for each policy you need to define.

    What is the difference between the **Account lockout duration** and the **Reset account lockout counter after** settings?

    _____

9. Close the Group Policy editor.

10. Click **OK** to close the domain properties.

2.3.5 DISABLE LAST LOGON NAME

Scenario

When you log on to a Windows computer, the last logon name you use is saved and then displayed the next time you try to log on. This can be a security concern because hackers can discover a valid user account name simply by looking at the logon screen. You can increase security by hiding the last logon name.

Your task in this lab is to force all computers in the domain to hide the last logon name.

- Edit the Default Domain policy linked to the domain.

- Enable the Computer Configuration\Windows Settings\Security Settings\Local Policies\ Security Options**Interactive logon: Do not display last user name in logon screen** policy.

Steps

Complete the following steps:

1. Click **Start/Administrative Tools/Active Directory Users and Computers**.

2. Right-click the domain and select **Properties**.

3. Click the **Group Policy** tab.

4. Select the **Default Domain Policy** GPO in the list, then click **Edit**.

5. Browse to **Computer Configuration\Windows Settings\Security Settings\Local Policies\ Security Options**.

6. Right-click the **Interactive logon: Do not display last user name in logon screen** policy and select **Properties**.

7. Click **Define this policy setting** and select **Enabled**. Click **OK**.

8. Close the Group Policy editor.

9. Click **OK** to close the domain properties.

2.3.7 MODIFY PASSWORD PROPERTIES

Scenario

You want to place stronger login restrictions on the user accounts in Shipping.Seattle.WestSim. Set the following restrictions for all user accounts in the Shipping.Seattle.WestSim container:

- Require passwords to be at least 8 characters long.

- Require the users to change their passwords every 30 days.

- Require unique passwords.

- Restrict the login time to between 6 a.m. and 6 p.m., Monday through Friday.

Steps

To configure login restrictions for all users in a container, edit the properties of the container, not each individual user object. In this scenario, edit the Shipping container properties.

Complete the following steps:

1. In ConsoleOne, expand the **WestSim-tree** node, the **WestSim** organization, and the **Seattle** OU.

2. Right-click the **Shipping** OU and select **Properties...**.

3. Click the **Restrictions** tab. The following dialog is shown.

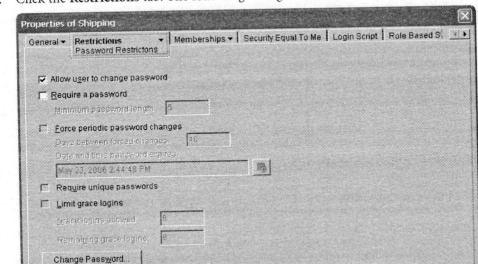

Make the following changes:

- Select **Require a password** and fill in the minimum password length.

- Select **Force periodic password changes** and fill in the **Days between forced changes** value.

- Select **Require unique passwords**.

4. Click the arrow next to the **Restrictions** tab and select **Time Restrictions**.

5. By default, access is allowed on all days and at all times. Select the boxes to identify times when log in is *not* allowed. **Tip:** Click and drag to select multiple boxes at once.

When you are finished, the dialog should resemble the following:

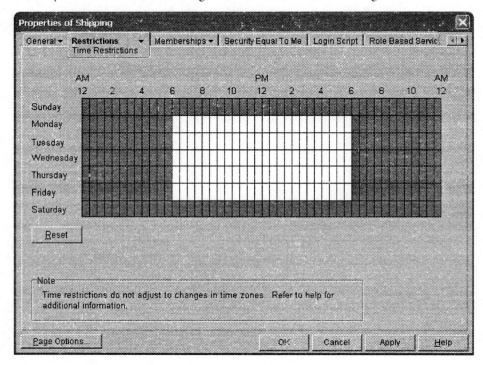

6. Click **OK** to save your changes.

2.3.8 RESTRICT LOGON HOURS

Scenario

Lynne Andersen is flying to Toronto to do some work there. Restrict the login time on the LAndersen.Production.Seattle.WestSim user object to allow login *only* between 6 a.m. and 10 p.m., Monday through Friday.

Steps

For this lab, edit the properties of the LAndersen.Production.Seattle.WestSim user object to set login restrictions for just that user.

Complete the following steps:

1. In ConsoleOne, expand the **WestSim-tree** node, the **WestSim** organization, and the **Seattle** OU. Click the **Production** container.

2. Right-click the **LAndersen** user object and select **Properties....**

3. Click the **Restrictions** tab.

4. Click the arrow next to the **Restrictions** tab and select **Time Restrictions.**

5. Select the boxes to identify times when log in is *not* allowed. **Tip:** Click and drag to select multiple boxes at once.

6. Click **OK** to save your changes.

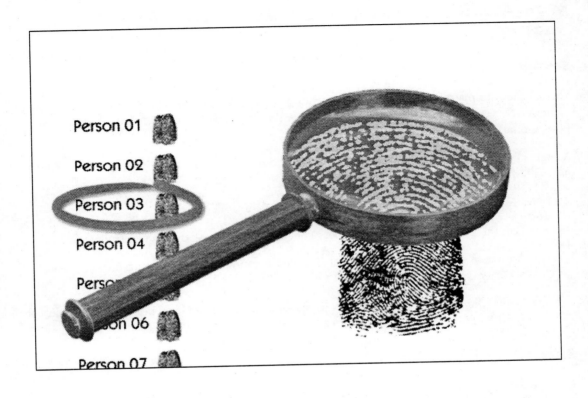

Person 01
Person 02
Person 03
Person 04
Person
on 06
Person 07

4.0

Authentication

4.1.5 ENFORCE NTLM AUTHENTICATION

Scenario

You are the administrator for the westsim.private domain. All servers run Windows 2000 Server or Windows Server 2003. All clients run Windows 98, Windows 2000 Professional, or Windows XP Professional.

As part of an increased security initiative, you want to make sure that all Windows 98 computers use NTLM v2 to authenticate to the domain.

Your task in this lab is to enforce NTLM v2 on domain controllers.

- Edit the Default Domain Controllers Policy (linked to the Domain Controllers OU).

- Browse to Computer Configuration/Windows Settings/Security Settings/Local Policies/ Security Options.

- Define the **Network security: LAN Manager authentication level** policy. Set the policy to **Send NTLMv2 response only\refuse LM & NTLM**.

Steps

Complete the following steps:

1. Click **Start/All Programs/Administrative Tools/Active Directory Users and Computers**.

2. Right-click the **Domain Controllers** node and choose **Properties** from the menu.

3. Click the **Group Policy** tab.

4. Select the Default **Domain Controllers Policy** and click **Edit**.

5. Browse to **Computer Configuration/Windows Settings/Security Settings/Local Policies/ Security Options**.

6. Right-click the **Network security: LAN Manager Authentication Level** policy and choose **Properties**. **Note:** Within the lab, the policy might not be in alphabetical order.

The following dialog box is shown.

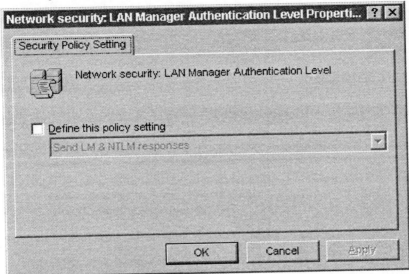

7. Select **Define this policy setting**, then select the desired authentication level. Click **OK**.

8. Close the Group Policy editor, then close the OU properties dialog.

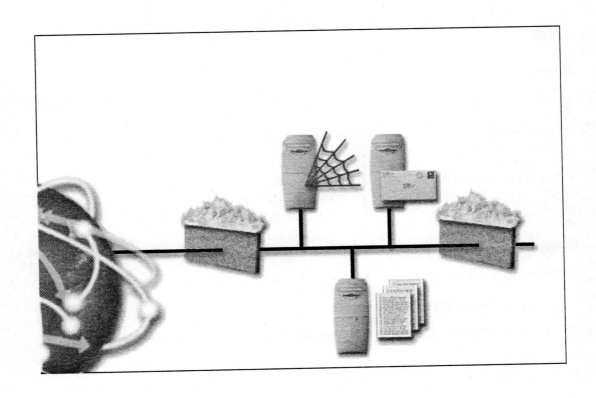

5.0

Network Infrastructure
Security

5.2.2 SHARE AN INTERNET CONNECTION

Scenario

You are configuring Internet connectivity for a small office network. You want all computers on the network to connect to the Internet using a shared dial-up network connection on a Windows XP Professional computer. You want the connection to be established automatically any time a computer tries to access the Internet.

Your task in this lab is to share the Dial Internet network connection on this computer. Allow on-demand dialing, but do not allow other users on the network to enable or disable the Internet connection manually.

Steps

Complete the following steps:

1. Click **Start/Control Panel**.

2. Click **Network and Internet Connections**.

3. Click the **Network Connections** icon.

4. Right-click the **Dial Internet** connection and select **Properties** from the menu.

5.   Click the **Advanced** tab. The following dialog is shown.

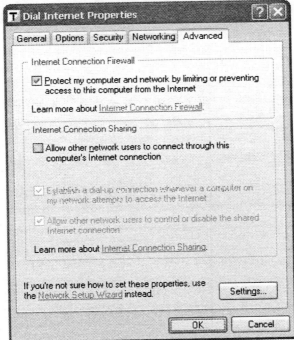

6.   Select the **Allow other network users to connect through this computer's Internet connection** option.

What must you do to enable the connection for use by all users?

_____

7.   Click **OK**.

Which option enabled on-demand dialing?

_____

8.   Deselect the **Allow other network users to control or disable the shared Internet connection** option.

9. Click **OK** to save the changes.

    What happens to the IP address of the LAN adapter when you enable connection sharing?

    _____

    What should you do to configure other computers on the network?

    _____

10. Click **Yes** to accept the changes.

5.2.4 CONFIGURE NAT

Scenario

You are configuring Internet access for a branch office. Workstations on the branch office's LAN will connect to the Internet through a Windows Server 2003 machine named Branch-Srv2. The relevant portion of the network is shown in the following graphic.

Your task in this lab is to use the Configure and Enable Routing and Remote Access wizard in Routing and Remote Access to configure the server as a NAT server.

- When the wizard starts, select **Network Address Translation (NAT)**.

- Create a demand-dial interface for the Internet connection. Use the 33.6 kbps modem for the port. Use the following property values when creating the demand-dial interface:

    ◦ Name = Dialup Internet

    ◦ Configure the connection to use the currently-installed modem

    ◦ Phone Number = 555-9834

    ◦ Protocols to route = IP (do *not* create a dial in user account)

    ◦ Dial out user name = Team45a

    ◦ Dial out password = study

- Accept the remaining NAT defaults (both DHCP and DNS services will be provided by other servers on the private network).

Steps

Complete the following steps:

1. Click **Start/Administrative Tools/Routing and Remote Access**.

2. Right click the server and select **Configure and Enable Routing and Remote Access**.

3. Click **Next** to start the Routing and Remote Access Server Setup wizard.

4. Select **Network address translation (NAT)** and click **Next**.

5. Because the dialup connection has not yet been defined in Routing and Remote Access, the **Create a new demand-dial Internet connection** option is already selected. Click **Next** to start the Routing and Remote Access and the Demand Dial Interface wizard.

6. Click **Next** to continue, then **Next** again to start the new wizard.

7. Type **Dialup Internet** for the interface name. Click **Next**.

8. Select the connection type. For this scenario, select **Connect using a modem, ISDN adapter, or other physical device**. Click **Next**.

9. Select the modem as the device to use, then click **Next**.

10. Enter in the phone number and click **Next**.

11. Accept the default protocols (**Route IP packets on this interface**) and click **Next**.

12. Type in the dial out user name and password. Click **Next**.

13. Click **Finish** to create the interface and enable it on the router.

14. Click **Finish** to close the Routing and Remote Access Server Setup wizard.

15. To see the effects of the configuration, expand the server node, expand the **IP Routing** node, then click the **NAT/Basic Firewall** node.

16. Right-click the **Local Area Connection** icon on the right and select **Properties**.

    What is the Interface Type configured for the connection?

    _____

17. Click **Cancel**.

18. Right-click the **Dialup Internet** icon and select **Properties**.

    What is the Interface Type configured for the connection?

    _____

19. Click **Cancel**.

5.3.5 ENABLE ICF

Scenario

You are configuring Internet connectivity for a small office network. All computers access the Internet through a shared dial-up connection on a Windows XP Professional computer. You want to protect the office network from malicious Internet users.

Your task in this lab is to enable Internet Connection Firewall (ICF) for the Dial Internet network connection on this computer. Keep the default ICF settings.

Steps

Complete the following steps:

1. Click **Start/Control Panel**.

2. Click **Network and Internet Connections**.

3. Click the **Network Connections** icon.

4. Right-click the **Dial Internet** connection and select **Properties** from the menu.

5. Click the **Advanced** tab.

6. To enable Internet Connection Firewall (ICF) for the network connection, select the **Protect my computer and network by limiting or preventing access to this computer from the Internet** option.

7. Click **OK** to save the changes to the network connection.

   How did the icon for the dialup connection change?

   _____

5.3.6 OPEN ICF PORTS

Scenario

You are configuring Internet connectivity for a small office network. A Windows XP Professional computer has two LAN adapters, one of which is named Broadband Internet and connects to the Internet using an always-on broadband connection. You have shared the Broadband Internet connection, and enabled Internet Connection Firewall (ICF) on the connection to protect the small office network from Internet users.

Users on the private network are able to access any Web site through the shared connection. However, Internet users cannot access the Web site that is hosted by the computer. The Web site is hosted over the default TCP port.

Your task in this lab is to allow Web communication from the Internet to this computer (LA-CORP-WRK3) by opening a port in the ICF firewall. Do not allow any other type of communication initiated from the Internet.

Steps

Complete the following steps:

1. Click **Start/Control Panel**.

2. Click **Network and Internet Connections**.

3. Click the **Network Connections** icon.

4. Right-click the **Broadband Internet** connection and select **Properties**.

5. Select the **Advanced** tab.

6. Click the **Settings...** button. The following dialog is shown.

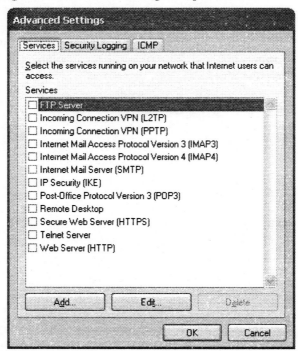

7.   Any listed service that is unchecked is blocked by the firewall. To allow a service, check the box next to it. In this scenario, check **Web Server (HTTP)**.

The following dialog is shown.

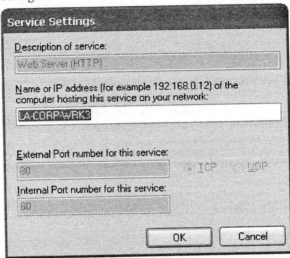

8.   Click **OK** to accept the default service settings.

9.   Click **OK**, then click **OK** again to save the settings.

5.3.7 CLOSE OPEN PORTS

Scenario

Your Windows XP Professional computer has two LAN adapters, one of which is named Broadband Internet and connects to the Internet using an always-on broadband connection. You have shared the Broadband Internet connection, and enabled Internet Connection Firewall (ICF) on the connection to protect the small office network from Internet users.

Previously, the workstation hosted a simple Web site for Internet users. You had opened ports in the firewall to allow HTTP and HTTPS traffic. You have since removed these services, and now you want to protect your computer by closing these ports.

Your task in this lab is to close all open ports in the Internet Connection Firewall.

Steps

Complete the following steps:

1. Click **Start/Control Panel**.

2. Click **Network and Internet Connections**.

3. Click the **Network Connections** icon.

4. Right-click the **Broadband Internet** connection and select **Properties**.

5. Select the **Advanced** tab.

6. Click the **Settings...** button.

7. Any listed service that is unchecked is blocked by the firewall. To secure the firewall, deselect all options.

8. Click **OK**, then click **OK** again to save the settings.

5.3.8 PREVENT ICMP EVENTS

Scenario

Your Windows XP Professional computer has two LAN adapters, one is named Broadband Internet and connects to the Internet using an always-on broadband connection. You have shared the Broadband Internet connection, and enabled Internet Connection Firewall (ICF) on the connection to protect the small office network from Internet users.

To run some tests, you enabled some ICMP messages in the firewall settings. Now, you want to disable all ICMP requests so that hackers can't use the Ping utility to probe your system and identify when your computer is online.

Your task in this lab is to edit the ICF settings to disallow all ICMP messages.

Steps

Complete the following steps:

1. Click **Start/Control Panel**.

2. Click **Network and Internet Connections**.

3. Click the **Network Connections** icon.

4. Right-click the **Broadband Internet** connection and select **Properties**.

5. Select the **Advanced** tab.

6. Click the **Settings...** button.

7. Click the **ICMP** tab. The following dialog is shown.

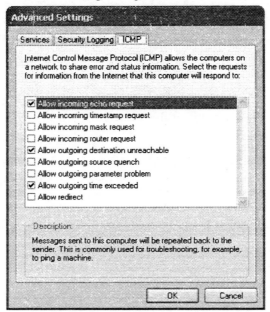

8. Select each ICMP message type to read a description about its function. In the following table, identify the ICMP message that performs the listed function.

Function	Message
Responds to requests for information about known routers	
Sends a message instructing the sending computer to slow down	
Responds when bad packets are received	
Allows a different path to be used if the default path changes	
Responds to ping messages	

9. To secure the firewall, uncheck all ICMP options.

10. Click **OK**, then click **OK** again to save the settings.

5.4.2 CREATE A PACKET FILTER 1

Scenario

The Corp-Rtr1 computer has two network connections as follows:

- The Local Area Connection interface connects to the private network. It has a network address of 67.101.150.62 with a mask of 255.255.255.224.

- The Internet interface connects to the Internet.

You want to prevent spoofed packets from being received from the Internet that claim to be coming from the private network. In Routing and Remote Access, define a packet filter on the Internet connection as follows:

- Create an inbound filter on the Internet connection.

- Create an exception to look for traffic from source network 67.101.150.62 with a mask of 255.255.255.224.

- Receive all packets except for those that meet the criteria.

Steps

Complete the following steps:

1. Click **Start/Administrative Tools/Routing and Remote Access**.

2. Expand the server object, expand the **IP Routing** node, then select the **General** node.

3. In the right window, right-click the **Internet** connection and click **Properties**.

4. On the **General** tab, click the **Inbound Filters...** button. The following dialog is shown.

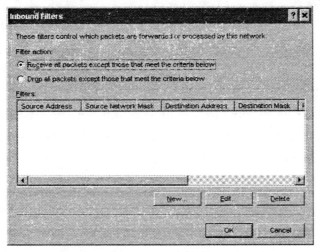

5. To create a filter rule, click **New....** The following dialog is shown.

6. Select **Source network** and type the IP address and mask. Click **OK**.

7. Make sure the **Receive all packets except those that meet the criteria below** option is selected. Click **OK** to finish creating the inbound filter.

8. Click **OK** to save the changes.

5.4.3 CREATE A PACKET FILTER 2

Scenario

The Corp-Rtr1 computer has two network connections as follows:

- The Local Area Connection interface connects to the private network. It has a network address of 67.101.150.62 with a mask of 255.255.255.224.

- The Internet interface connects to the Internet.

The router has been the victim of several Denial of Service attacks from a specific host (address 188.97.155.12). You have decided to simply block all traffic coming from this host to reduce the processing required for the router. In Routing and Remote Access, define a packet filter on the Internet connection as follows:

- Create an inbound filter on the Internet connection.

- Create an exception to look for traffic from source host 188.97.155.12 with a mask of 255.255.255.255.

- Receive all packets except for those that meet the criteria.

Steps

Complete the following steps:

1. Click **Start/Administrative Tools/Routing and Remote Access**.

2. Expand the server object, expand the **IP Routing** node, then select the **General** node.

3. In the right window, right-click the **Internet** connection and click **Properties**.

4. On the **General** tab, click the **Inbound Filters...** button.

5. To create a filter rule, click **New....**

6. Select **Source network** and type the IP address and mask. Click **OK**.

7. Make sure the **Receive all packets except those that meet the criteria below** option is selected. Click **OK** to finish creating the inbound filter.

8. Click **OK** to save the changes.

5.4.5 APPLY ACCESS LISTS TO INTERFACES

Scenario

Standard access lists have been configured on the Lisbon router. Apply access lists to various interfaces as follows:

- Ethernet0. Access list 1 to control inbound traffic; access list 15 to control outbound traffic.

- Serial0. Access list 15 to control inbound traffic; access list 99 to control outbound traffic.

- Serial1. Access list 22 to control outbound traffic.

Steps

Complete the following steps:

1. Click the router icon to open the router console.

2. Press **Enter**.

3. Type the enable command.

4. Type the following command to enter configuration mode: `configure terminal`

5. To enter configuration mode for the Ethernet interface, type: `interface ethernet0`

6. Use the following commands to apply the access lists to the interface:

   ```
   ip access-group 1 in
   ip access-group 15 out
   ```

   What do the **in** and **out** parameters indicate?

   _____

7.   To enter configuration mode for the first serial interface, type: **`interface serial0`**

8.   Use the following commands to apply the access lists to the interface:

```
ip access-group 15 in
ip access-group 99 out
```

9.   To enter configuration mode for the second serial interface, type: **`interface serial1`**

10. To apply the access list to the interface, type: **`ip access-group 22 out`**

11. Press Ctrl + Z to exit configuration mode.

5.4.6 RESTRICT TRAFFIC FROM SPECIFIC HOSTS

Scenario

For the Fiji router, create a standard IP access list (numbered 66) with statements that do the following:

- Deny traffic from host 1.1.2.12

- Deny traffic from host 2.16.11.155

- Allow all other traffic

When you are finished, apply the list to Ethernet0 to prevent the traffic defined by the list from being sent out the interface.

Tip: Each restriction above requires one access-list statement. You should have three statements when you are finished.

Steps

Complete the following steps:

1. Click the router icon to open the router console.

2. Press **Enter**.

3. Type the **enable** command.

4. Type the following command to enter configuration mode: `configure terminal`

5. Define the access list using the following commands:

    ```
    access-list 66 deny 1.1.2.12
    access-list 66 deny 2.16.11.155
    access-list 66 permit any
    ```

6. With the access list defined, you need to apply it to an interface. Use the following command to enter configuration mode for the Ethernet interface: **interface ethernet0**

7. Apply the access list with the following command: **ip access-group 66 out**

8. Press Ctrl + Z to exit configuration mode.

5.4.7 RESTRICT TRAFFIC FROM SPECIFIC NETWORKS

Scenario

Create access list 53 on the Fiji router that permits all traffic except from the following networks:

- network 10.244.0.0 with mask 255.255.0.0

- network 172.16.200.0 with mask 255.255.255.0

Apply the list to the first Ethernet interface to restrict outgoing traffic.

Note: When creating an access control list to restrict traffic from a network, you need to use a wildcard mask to identify the network. The wildcard mask is the reverse of the subnet mask. For the networks in this scenario, use the following mask values:

- 10.244.0.0 0.0.255.255

- 172.16.200.0 0.0.0.255

Steps

Complete the following steps:

1. Click the router icon to open the router console.

2. Press **Enter**.

3. Type the **enable** command.

4. Type the following command to enter configuration mode: `configure terminal`

5. Define the access list using the following commands:

```
access-list 53 deny 10.244.0.0 0.0.255.255
access-list 53 deny 172.16.200.0 0.0.0.255
access-list 53 permit any
```

6.   With the access list defined, you need to apply it to an interface. Use the following command to enter configuration mode for the Ethernet interface: `interface ethernet0`

7.   Apply the access list with the following command: `ip access-group 53 out`

8.   Press Ctrl + Z to exit configuration mode.

5.5.2 CREATE A VLAN AND ASSIGN PORTS

Scenario

Complete the following tasks:

1. Create VLAN 6 on the switch.

2. Assign the switch ports connected to Wrk2 and Wrk4 to this VLAN.

Steps

Complete the following steps:

1. Click the switch icon to open the console.

2. Press **Enter**.

3. Type the **enable** command.

4. Type the following command to enter configuration mode: `configure terminal`

5. Use the following command to define the VLAN: `vlan 6`

6. To assign a switch port to a VLAN, start by switching to configuration mode for the port using the following command: `interface FastEthernet0/2`

7. Assign the port to the VLAN using the following command: `switchport access vlan 6`

8. Repeat steps 6 and 7 to assign additional ports to the VLAN.

9. Press Ctrl + Z to exit configuration mode.

5.5.3 EXPLORING VLAN COMMUNICATION

Scenario

In this lab, you will explore how VLAN membership effects device communications. The LAN is configured as shown in the diagram, with all switch ports up and assigned to the default VLAN (VLAN 1).

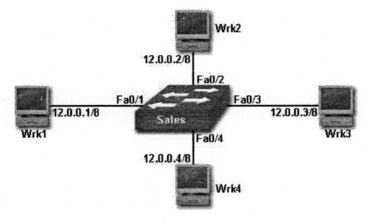

Steps

Complete the following steps:

1. Click the Wrk1 icon to open a command prompt on the workstation.

2. Use the **ping** command to verify that Wrk1 can communicate with all other workstations on the network. Record the results in the table below.

Ping Command	Result
ping 12.0.0.2	
ping 12.0.0.3	
ping 12.0.0.4	

3. Click the switch icon to open its console, then press **Enter**.

4. Type the **enable** command.

5. Use the **configure terminal** command to enter configuration mode.

6. Create VLAN 12 using the following command: **vlan 12**

7. Enter interface configuration mode using the **interface fastethernet0/1** command.

8. Assign port 0/1 to VLAN 12 with the following command: **switchport access vlan 12**

9. Click the Wrk1 icon to open the command prompt on the workstation.

10. Use the **ping** command to test connectivity with the other workstations on the network. Record the results in the following table.

Ping Command	Result
ping 12.0.0.2	
ping 12.0.0.3	
ping 12.0.0.4	

Why has the workstation's ability to communicate on the network changed?

_____

11. Click the switch icon to return to its console.

12. Use the following commands to assign port 0/3 to VLAN 12:

```
interface fastethernet0/3
switchport access vlan 12
```

13. Click the Wrk1 icon to open the command prompt on the workstation.

14. Use the **ping** command to test connectivity with the other workstations on the network. Record the results in the following table.

Ping Command	Result
ping 12.0.0.2	
ping 12.0.0.3	
ping 12.0.0.4	

What has changed? Why?

_____

6.0

Network and
Application Hardening

6.2.4 DISABLE FILE AND PRINTER SHARING

Scenario

Your Windows XP Professional computer has a dialup connection to the Internet. In a recent article, you read about hackers who are able to access system resources because File and Printer Sharing is enabled on computers connected to the Internet.

Your task in this lab is to disable File and Printer Sharing on the Internet connection. Disable the Microsoft Client component as well. Do *not* uninstall these components. Do not change the settings for the LAN connection.

Steps

To disable a component on a connection, edit the connection properties. On the Networking tab, uncheck the box next to the component you want to disable. This leaves the component installed on the computer and still in use by other connections.

Complete the following steps:

1. Click **Start/Network Connections**.

2. Right-click the connection and select **Properties** from the menu.

3. Click the **Networking** tab. The following dialog is shown.

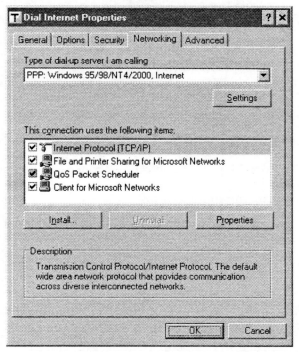

4. In the list of components, deselect the component you want to disable (clear the check box next to the component). Click **OK**.

5. To verify that the LAN connection protocols have not changed, right-click the Local Area Connection and choose **Properties**. Verify that the File and Printer Sharing and Microsoft Client components are still enabled for the LAN connection.

6.2.5 UNINSTALL A COMPONENT

Scenario

Your network has just finished the migration from NetWare to an all Windows Server 2003 network. During the migration, you had the NetWare client software installed on some of the servers. Now that the migration is over, you want to remove any client software and protocols used by NetWare.

Your task in this lab is to uninstall the Client Services for NetWare component.

Steps

Your task in this lab is to uninstall the Client Services for NetWare component. When you uninstall the client software, the protocols that the client software uses are removed automatically. To remove the client component, edit the LAN adapter properties and remove the software.

Complete the following steps:

1. Click **Start/Network Connections**.

2. Right-click **Local Area Connection** and choose **Properties** from the menu.

    What components are currently installed?

    _____

    _____

    _____

    _____

    _____

3. Highlight the **Client Service for NetWare** component.

4. Click **Uninstall**.

5. Click **Yes** to confirm the uninstall.

    What would you typically need to do to complete the component uninstall?

    _____

6. Click **OK**.

    Which components were removed?

    _____

    _____

    _____

6.2.6 DISABLE NETBIOS OVER TCP/IP

Scenario

You are the administrator of a small network that uses only Windows Server 2003 on the servers and Windows XP Professional on clients. The network has a DHCP server, but several of the servers have static IP addresses.

Because all clients can use DNS for name resolution, you want to minimize the protocols running on each computer.

Your task in this lab is to disable NetBIOS over TCP/IP on the server. (To do this, edit the Advanced TCP/IP properties and use the settings on the WINS tab.)

Steps

NetBIOS over TCP/IP is only used to find NetBIOS-named hosts on the network. If your network has clients that support DNS (such as all Windows 2000/XP/2003), you can disable NetBIOS over TCP/IP. To do this, edit the Advanced TCP/IP properties. On the WINS tab, disable NetBIOS over TCP/IP.

Complete the following steps:

1.   Click **Start/Network Connections**.

2.   Right-click the **Local Area Connection** node and choose **Properties** from the menu.

3.   Select the **Internet Protocol (TCP/IP)** network. Click **Properties**.

4.   Click the **Advanced...** button.

5.   Click the **WINS** tab. The following dialog is shown.

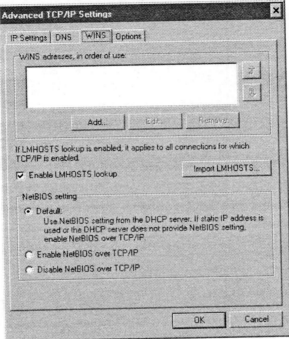

6.   Select **Disable NetBIOS over TCP/IP**. Click **OK**.

7.   Click **OK**, then **OK** again to close all dialog boxes.

6.2.9 ENFORCE SMB SIGNING

Scenario

You are the administrator for the westsim.private domain. All servers in the domain run Windows Server 2003. Clients run Windows 98, Windows 2000 Professional, or Windows XP Professional.

Your security policy calls for secure communications between all computers on your network. Because Windows 98 does not support IPSec, you decide to enforce SMB signing for all network communications.

Your task in this lab is to enforce SMB signing through the use of a GPO.

- Use Active Directory Users and Computers to edit the Default Domain Policy GPO (linked to the westsim.private domain).

- Browse to Computer Configuration/Windows Settings/Security Settings/Local Policies/ Security Options.

- Enable the **Microsoft network client: Digitally sign communications (always)** policy.

- Enable the **Microsoft network server: Digitally sign communications (always)** policy.

- Edit the Default Domain Controllers Policy (linked to the Domain Controllers OU) and enable the **Microsoft network client: Digitally sign communications (always)** policy. (The server setting is already enabled by the GPO.)

Note: Group Policy will not apply to the Windows 98 computers. You will need to manually enforce SMB signing on each Windows 98 client. However, this task is not required as part of the lab.

Steps

Complete the following steps:

1. Click **Start/All Programs/Administrative Tools/Active Directory Users and Computers**.

2. Right-click the domain and choose **Properties** from the menu.

3. Click the **Group Policy** tab.

4. Select the **Default Domain Policy** and click **Edit**.

5. Browse to **Computer Configuration/Windows Settings/Security Settings/Local Policies/Security Options**.

6. Double-click the policy you want to edit.

7. Check **Define this policy setting**, then select **Enabled**. Click **OK**.

8. Repeat steps 6 and 7 to define additional policies.

9. Close the Group Policy Object Editor.

10. Click **OK** to close the domain properties dialog.

11. Right-click the **Domain Controllers** node and choose **Properties** from the menu.

12. Click the **Group Policy** tab.

13. Select the **Default Domain Controllers Policy** and click **Edit**.

14. Browse to **Computer Configuration/Windows Settings/Security Settings/Local Policies/Security Options**.

15. Double-click the policy you want to configure.

16. Check **Define this policy setting** and click **Enabled**. Click **OK**.

17. Close the **Group Policy Object Editor** dialog.

18. Click **OK** to close the OU properties dialog.

6.3.7 STOP AND DISABLE SERVICES

Scenario

The Sea-IT-Srv1 server provides Web services for your company. You want to harden the server by removing unnecessary services.

For each of the service listed here, stop the service (if it is running) and change the startup type to *Disabled*.

- DNS Server

- Messenger

- Novell Application Launcher

- Novell Workstation Manager

- TCP/IP NetBIOS Helper

Steps

Complete the following steps:

1. Click **Start/Administrative Tools/Services** to open the Services console.

    Which of the following services are currently started? (Examine at the **Status** column in the console.)

Alerter	DHCP Client	DNS Client
Fax Service	HTTP SSL	Indexing Service

2. Right-click the service that you want to stop and choose **Stop** from the menu. Repeat this step for any additional services you want to disable.

    Even though you have stopped the unnecessary services, they might still be configured to start automatically the next time the server restarts. The state of the service is controlled by the startup type. You can view the startup type for each service in the console by expanding the console window and looking at the **Startup Type** column.

What is the current startup type for each of the following services?

Service	Startup Type
ClipBook	
Internet Connection Sharing	
Net Logon	
Plug and Play	
Routing and Remote Access	

3. To configure the startup behavior, double-click the service. The following dialog is shown.

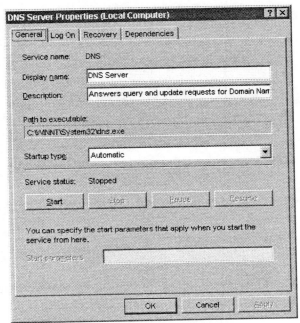

4. In the **Startup type:** drop-down list, select **Disabled**, then click **OK**.

5. Repeat steps 3 and 4 to modify additional services.

6.4.2 FORMAT A DRIVE

Scenario

You have just installed a new hard disk in the server and created a volume on that disk. The volume name is Data2 and the drive letter is E:.

After you create the volume, you notice that it was formatted with FAT32. You want the volume to use NTFS so that you can use NTFS permissions and encryption. The drive does not yet contain any data.

Your task in this lab is to format the E: drive with NTFS.

Steps

Complete the following steps:

1. Click **Start/My Computer**.

2. Right-click the drive and select **Format...** from the menu. The following dialog is shown.

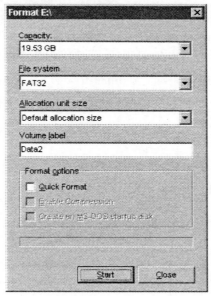

3. Select the file system type and click **Start**.

    What happens to existing data on the drive when you format it?

    _____

4. Click **OK** to continue, then **OK** to finish.

6.4.3 CONVERT A DRIVE

Scenario

You are the administrator for the SEA-IT-SRV1 server. The Data volume (drive D:) is used to hold shared data for the Accounting workgroup. You have begun copying files to the D: drive.

When you go to set NTFS permissions on certain folders, the Security tab is not available for any folder on the volume. You realize that the volume has been formatted with FAT32.

Your task in this lab is to convert the Data volume (drive D:) to NTFS using the **Convert.exe** utility.

Steps

Complete the following steps:

1. Click **Start/Command Prompt**.

2. Type **convert /?** to see a list of options for the command.

    What does the **/V** switch do?

    _____

    What does the **/X** switch do?

    _____

3. Type **convert d: /fs:ntfs**.

4. You will be prompted to enter the volume label. To find the volume label, click **Start/My Computer**. The volume label will be listed before the drive letter (D:).

5. Return to the command prompt window and type the volume label. Press Enter.

6.4.5 CHANGE NTFS PERMISSIONS

Scenario

The Sea-IT-Srv1 server is a file server that holds files used by all users in the company. Two folders have been created and shared on the D:\ drive: Reports and Suggestions.

Current NTFS permissions allow all users to read and view files in both folders. However, users need to be able to save files to the Suggestions folder and change existing files.

Your task in this lab is to grant the Users group the Allow Modify permission to the D:\ Suggestions folder.

Steps

Complete the following steps:

1. Click **Start/My Computer**.

2. Begin by viewing the NTFS permissions assigned to the D: drive. Right-click the drive and select **Properties** from the menu.

3. Click the **Security** tab. The following dialog is shown.

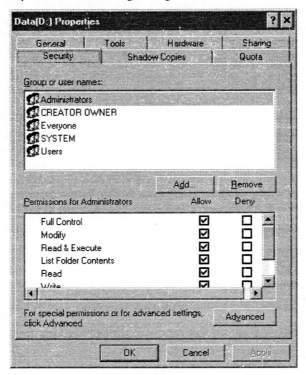

Selecting a user or a group in the top box displays the NTFS permissions in the bottom box. What NTFS permissions have been assigned to the following groups?

Group	NTFS Permissions
Administrators	
Everyone	
Users	

4. Click **Cancel** to close the drive properties.

5. Double-click the D: drive.

6. Right-click the **Suggestions** folder and choose **Properties** from the menu.

7. Click the **Security** tab.

    Notice that the permissions for all groups are greyed out. This indicates that permissions have been inherited from the parent drive or folders.

8. To modify the permissions, click the **Advanced** button. The following dialog is shown.

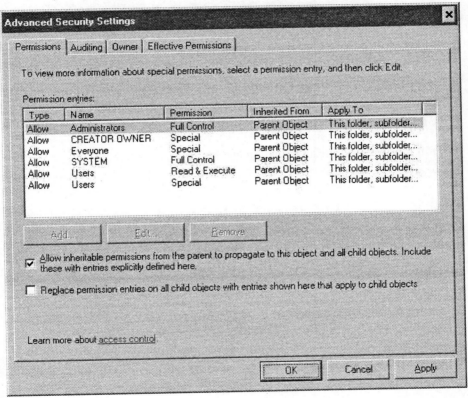

9. Deselect **Allow inheritable permissions from the parent to propagate to this object and all child object**. The following dialog is shown.

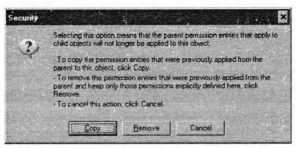

10. Click **Copy**.

11. Click **OK**.

What has happened to the permission entries for each group?

_____

12. Select the **Users** group, then click the **Modify** permission in the Allow column.

What other permission is also granted when you grant Modify?

_____

13. Click **OK** to save the changes.

6.4.6 CONFIGURE NTFS PERMISSIONS

Scenario

You are configuring the file system of a Windows Server 2003 computer. Currently, all users can view the data on the D:\ drive, but only administrators can change or delete the data. You want to keep these permissions, but also allow members of the Research domain global group to change and delete the contents of the drive.

Your task in this lab is to configure NTFS permissions so that members of the Research domain global group can view and change the contents of the D:\ drive (grant the Allow Modify permission).

Steps

Complete the following steps:

1. Click **Start/My Computer**.

2. Right-click the D: drive and select **Properties**.

3. Click the **Security** tab.

4. To add a user or group to the access control list (ACL), click the **Add...** button. The following dialog is shown.

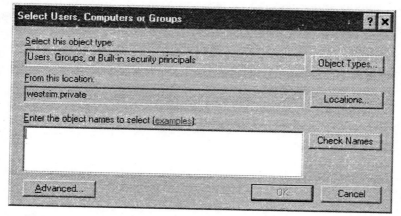

5. Type **Research** and click **OK**.

6. Select the **Research** group and click **OK**.

   What are the default permissions assigned to the group when it is added to the ACL?

   _____

7. Click the **Modify** permission in the Allow column to grant additional permissions.

8. Click **OK** to save the changes.

6.4.8 ENCRYPT A FILE

Scenario

You are a consultant for a security firm. Your latest client has requested a security audit of their systems and processes. You have completed the analysis, and are preparing to give your final report. The company has several governmental contracts, and you want to make sure that your security audit cannot be read if you lose your laptop.

Your task in this lab is to encrypt the C:\Documents and Settings\Administrator\My Documents\Work\Security Report.doc file. No other files should be encrypted.

Steps

Complete the following steps:

1. Click **Start/My Computer**.

2. In Windows Explorer, browse to the desired folder or file.

3. Right-click **Security Report.doc** file and choose **Properties** from the menu.

4. Click the **Advanced...** button. The following dialog is shown.

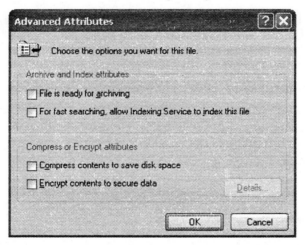

5. Select the **Encrypt contents to secure data** option. Then select the **Encrypt contents to secure data** option.

   What happens to the compression setting?

   _____

6. Click **OK**.

7. Click **OK** again.

8. Select **Encrypt the file only**, then click **OK**.

6.4.9 ENCRYPT A FOLDER AND CONTENTS

Scenario

You have a laptop computer that you use in a docking station at work as well as on the road. You are the manager for your department, and frequently store employee evaluations and research results on your laptop. You want to protect your sensitive files from others. You have created the C:\Confidential folder and moved all files into that folder.

Your task in this lab is to encrypt the C:\Confidential folder, all its files, and all files that will be stored there.

Steps

Complete the following steps:

1. Click **Start/My Computer**.

2. In Windows Explorer, browse to the desired folder or file.

3. Right-click **C:\Confidential** folder and choose **Properties** from the menu.

4. Click the **Advanced...** button.

5. Select **Encrypt contents to secure data**. Click **OK**.

6. Click **OK** again.

7. Select **Apply changes to this folder, subfolders, and files**, then click **OK**.

6.5.2 MODIFY FILE SYSTEM RIGHTS

Scenario

The Graphics group in the Production.Seattle.WestSim container is a trustee of the WS-SRV2_ Shares.Seattle.WestSim:/Projects and Testing directories. You've found out that some members of the Graphics group make changes to files after they've been placed in the Testing directory.

On the WS-SRV2_Shares.Seattle.WestSim:/Testing directory, remove the **Write**, **Create**, **Erase**, and **Modify** rights from the Graphics.Production.Seattle.WestSim group.

Steps

Complete the following steps:

1. In ConsoleOne, expand **WestSim-tree** and **WestSim**. Click the **Seattle** OU.

2. Double-click the **WS-SRV2_Shares** volume.

3. Right-click the **Testing** directory and select **Properties...** from the menu.

4. Click the **Trustees** tab. The following dialog is shown.

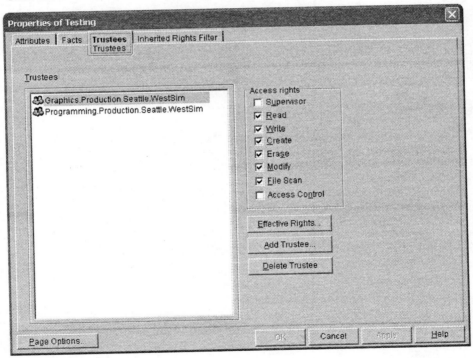

5. Make sure the **Graphics.Production.Seattle.WestSim** group is selected. Deselect the rights that you want to revoke.

6. Click **OK**.

6.5.3 ADD A TRUSTEE AND RIGHTS

Scenario

Armando Gonzales has responsibility for the information in the Personnel directory. Make AGonzales.Executive.Seattle.WestSim a trustee of the WS-SRV2_Shares.Seattle.WestSim:/Personnel directory. Grant him Supervisor rights.

Steps

You can make a file system trustee assignment through a directory or file, or you can make the trustee assignment through the container, group, or user object. **Tip:** Make the assignment through the container, group, or user object if you're assigning rights to several directories or files at once to that object.

Complete the following steps:

1. In ConsoleOne, expand **WestSim-tree** and **WestSim**. Click the **Seattle** OU.

2. Double-click the **WS-SRV2_Shares** volume.

3. Right-click the **Personnel** folder and select **Properties....**

4. Click the **Trustees** tab. The following dialog is shown.

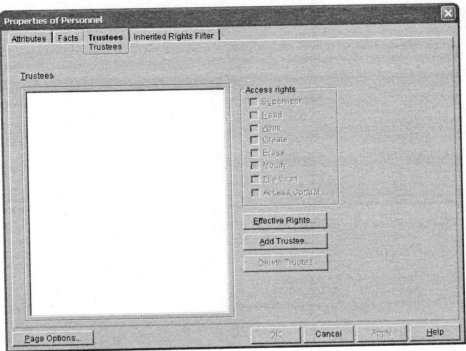

5. Click the **Add Trustee...** button. The following dialog is shown.

6. Double-click **WestSim**, double-click **Seattle**, then double-click **Executive**. Select the **AGonzales** object and click **OK**.

What are the default rights assigned to AGonzales?

_____

7. Click the rights to assign to the user. Click **OK**.

6.5.5 MODIFY FOLDER ATTRIBUTES

Scenario

You keep important files for system maintenance in the Applications/Utilities subdirectory on the WS-SRV2_Shares.Seattle.WestSim volume. Consequently, you want to control the operations that can be performed on the files in that directory.

Set the following directory attributes on the Utilities directory:

- Delete Inhibit
- Rename Inhibit
- Hidden

Steps

Complete the following steps:

1. In ConsoleOne, expand **WestSim-tree** and **WestSim**. Click the **Seattle** OU.

2. Double-click the **WS-SRV2_Shares** volume, then double-click the **Applications** folder.

3. Right-click the **Utilities** folder and select **Properties…**. The following dialog is shown.

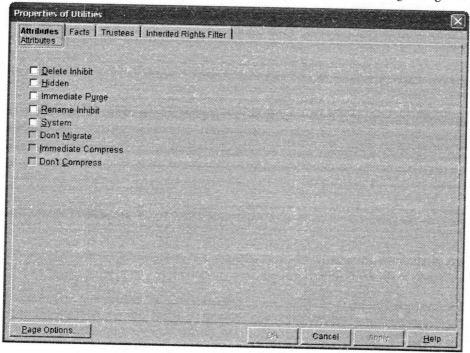

4. Select the required folder attributes. Click **OK**.

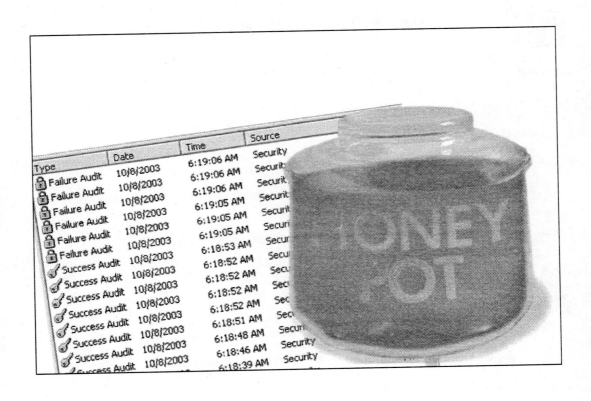

Auditing and Intrusion Detection

7.1.4 ENABLE AUDITING 1

Scenario

You are a network administrator for your company. Your company has a single Active Directory domain named westsim.private. As part of securing the domain, you want to detect all failed attempts to log on to the domain.

Enable auditing of the appropriate event to meet the above requirement.

- Configure auditing on the Default Domain Controllers Policy linked to the Domain Controllers OU.

- Enable the Account Logon Events policy to catch unsuccessful attempts.

Steps

Complete the following steps:

1. Click **Start/Administrative Tools/Active Directory Users and Computers.**

2. Right-click the **Domain Controllers** OU and select **Properties.**

3. Click the **Group Policy** tab.

4. Select the **Default Domain Controllers Policy** GPO, then click **Edit.**

5. Browse to **Computer Configuration/Windows Settings/Security Settings/Local Policies/ Audit Policy.**

6. Double-click the **Audit account logon** events policy. The following dialog is shown.

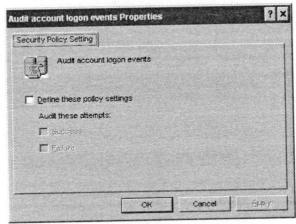

7. Select **Define these policy settings**. Because you only want to catch failed events, select only **Failure**. Click **OK**.

8. Close the Group Policy editor.

9. Click **OK** to close the OU properties.

7.1.5 ENABLE AUDITING 2

Scenario

You have noticed some changes being made to domain controllers on your network. When you confront your other system administrators, they all deny having made any changes. You want to implement auditing to track startup and shutdown, changing the system time, and changing user rights on the domain controllers.

Your task in this lab is to configure auditing as follows:

- Configure auditing on the Default Domain Controllers Policy linked to the Domain Controllers OU.

- Enable the Policy Change policy to catch successful actions.

- Enable the System Events policy to catch successful actions.

Steps

Complete the following steps:

1. Click **Start/Administrative Tools/Active Directory Users and Computers**.

2. Right-click the **Domain Controllers** OU and select **Properties**.

3. Click the **Group Policy** tab.

4. Select the **Default Domain Controllers Policy** GPO, then click **Edit**.

5. Browse to **Computer Configuration/Windows Settings/Security Settings/Local Policies/Audit Policy**.

6. Double-click the audit policy you want to enable.

7. Select **Define these policy settings** and select either **Success** or **Failure** (or both). Click **OK**.

8. Repeat steps 6 and 7 to configure any additional policies.

9. Close the Group Policy editor.

10. Click **OK** to close the OU properties.

7.1.7 SAVE THE AUDIT LOG

Scenario

In response to some suspicious activity on your network, you have enabled auditing on one of your file servers. After looking at the auditing entries, you think you notice some audit entries that identify an employee that has been performing some malicious activities. You now need to archive the audit log to preserve the data for further analysis and possible prosecution.

Your task in this lab is to clear the Security log and save its contents to D:\Confidential\Logfile1.evt.

Steps

Complete the following steps:

1. Click **Start/Administrative Tools/Event Viewer**.

2. Right-click the **Security** node and select **Clear all Events**.

3. Click **Yes** to save the log.

4. Double-click the **D:** drive, then double-click the **Confidential** folder.

5. Type the log file name and click **Save**.

   Even though you cleared the log, why is there still an event shown on the right? (**Tip:** Right-click the event and choose **Properties** to read the event description.)

   _____

   How does this action increase the security of your logs?

   _____

7.1.8 CHANGE LOG PROPERTIES

Scenario

Recently, you have noticed some suspicious activity on your network. You are concerned that someone is trying to log on to one of your network servers. You have enabled auditing to catch unsuccessful logon attempts. You want to make sure that the Security Log can handle the volume of events that might be generated. You also want to make sure that no important events in the log are overwritten when the log fills up.

Your task in this lab is to:

- Increase the maximum size for the Security log to 248000 KB.

- Configure the Security log to never overwrite events.

Steps

Complete the following steps:

1. Click **Start/Administrative Tools/Event Viewer**.

2. Right-click the **Security** node and select **Properties**. The following dialog is shown.

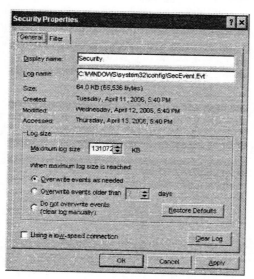

3. Modify the log size and the log behavior as required.

   What must you do if you configure the log to never overwrite events?

   _____

4. Click **OK** to save your changes.

7.1.9 CONFIGURE THE SYSTEM TO SHUT DOWN

Scenario

You have recently enabled auditing on the domain controllers in your organization. You have also configured the Security log to never overwrite events. However, you discover that when the event log gets full, the new audit entries are simply not recorded. This means that malicious activity that happens after the event log fills up could go unaudited. You want to configure the domain controllers to shut down when the audit log fills up.

Your task in this lab is to force the domain controllers to shut down when the event logs are full. Take the following steps:

1. 1. In Active Directory Users and Computers, edit the Default Domain Controllers policy (linked to the Domain Controllers OU).

2. 2. Enable the following policy: **Computer Configuration\Windows Settings\Security Settings\Local Policies\Security Options\Audit: Shut down system immediately if unable to log security audits.**

Steps

Complete the following steps:

1. Click **Start/Administrative Tools/Active Directory Users and Computers**.

2. Right-click the **Domain Controllers** OU and select **Properties**.

3. Click the **Group Policy** tab.

4. Select the **Default Domain Controllers Policy** GPO, then click **Edit**.

5. Browse to **Computer Configuration\Windows Settings\Security Settings\Local Policies\ Security Options**.

6. Double-click the **Audit: Shut down system immediately if unable to log security audits** policy.

7. Select **Define this policy setting**, then select **Enabled**. Click **OK**.

8. Close the Group Policy editor.

9. Click **OK** to close the OU properties.

8.0

Communication
Security

8.1.4 CONFIGURE A REMOTE ACCESS SERVER

Scenario

You have installed a new Windows Server 2003 computer named branch-Srv1. You now want to configure the server to allow remote access. A DHCP server is currently operating on the network and will be used to supply addresses for remote clients. RADIUS authentication and accounting will *not* be used.

Your task in this lab is to use Routing and Remote Access to configure the Branch-Srv1 server as a remote access server.

Steps

Use the Configure and Enable Routing and Remote Access Server wizard to configure the server. When the wizard starts, select the **Remote access (dial-up or VPN)** option.

Complete the following steps:

1. Click **Start/Administrative Tools/Routing and Remote Access** to open the Routing and Remote Access snap-in.

2. Right-click the server and choose **Configure and Enable Routing and Remote Access** from the menu.

3. Click **Next** to start the wizard.

4. Select **Remote access (dial-up or VPN)** and click **Next**.

5. Check the **Dial-up** option and click **Next**.

6. Verify that **Automatically** is selected for DHCP configuration for the remote access server. Click **Next**.

7. Verify that RADIUS is not used. Click **Next**.

8. Click **Finish** to complete the configuration. The modem will be automatically enabled to accept remote access connections.

9. To verify the configuration, right-click the server and select **Properties**.

   Which option is selected on the **General** tab?

   _____

10. Click **Cancel**.

8.1.6 CREATE A REMOTE ACCESS POLICY

Scenario

You have configured the Branch-Srv1 server as a remote access server to allow dial-in connections through its modem. Members of the Sales team will connect to the remote access server to enter in daily orders and check on order status.

Your task in this lab is to configure a remote access policy to allow members of the Sales team to connect. Complete the following tasks:

1. Create a remote access policy called *Sales*. Use the wizard to create the remote access policy.

2. Choose **Dial-up** as the access method.

3. Identify access using members of the Sales group.

4. Accept only EAP with smart cards for authentication.

5. Allow Basic, Strong, or Strongest encryption.

6. Make sure the policy is first in the list of policies.

After you have created the policy, use Active Directory Users and Computers to edit the following user accounts to enable dial-in permission (edit the setting on the Dial-in tab of each user account):

- Sam Charles

- Sandy Santos

- Sally Smith

- Wanda Lewis

- Will Adams

Steps

Complete the following steps:

1. Click **Start/Administrative Tools/Routing and Remote Access**.

2. Expand the server node.

3. Right-click the Remote Access Policies node and select **New Remote Access Policy**.

4. Click **Next** to start the wizard.

5. Type the name for the remote access policy. Click **Next**.

6. Select **Dial-up** as the access method. This adds Async (Modem) and all ISDN options to the policy *conditions*. Click **Next**.

7. Select **Group**, then click **Add...** to add the Sales group.

8. Type **Sales** for the group name and click **OK**. This adds membership in the Sales group as a policy *condition*.

9. Click **Next** to continue.

10. Select **Extensible Authentication Protocol (EAP)** as the authentication type. Choose **Smart Card or other certificate** as the EAP method. Deselect any other protocols. This adds EAP to the *profile*. The completed dialog should look as follows:

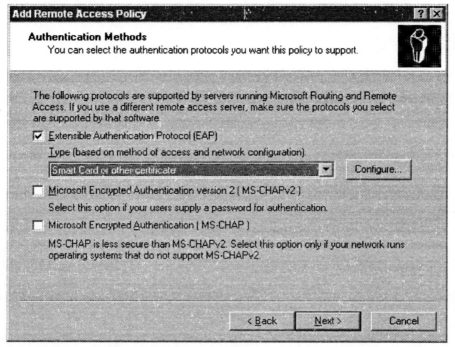

Under which condition would adding MS-CHAP as a protocol be acceptable?

_____

11. Click **Next** to continue.

12. Verify that the encryption settings are correct. Encryption methods are added to the *profile*. Click **Next**.

13. Click **Finish**.

14. Next you must configure remote access permissions in the necessary user accounts. To do so, click **Start/Administrative Tools/Active Directory Users and Computers**.

15. Click the Sales OU.

16. Right-click a user account and select **Properties**.

17. Click the **Dial-in** tab. The following dialog is shown.

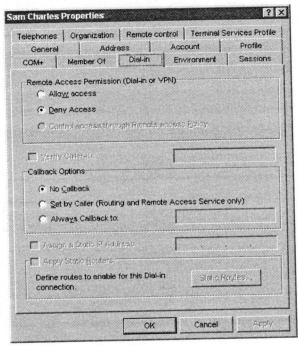

18. Select **Allow access**. Click **OK**.

19. Repeat steps 16 through 18 for additional user accounts.

8.1.8 CREATE A DIALUP CONNECTION

Scenario

You need to configure a workstation at a branch office to access your company's main network remotely over a dial-up connection. The workstation is a Windows XP Professional computer.

Your task in this lab is to use the New Connection wizard in Network and Dial-up Connections to create a dialup connection on the workstation.

- When the wizard starts, select **Connect to the network at my workplace**.

- Name the connection *Main Office*.

- Configure it to dial the phone number *555-9862*.

After the connection is created, edit the properties of the connection and configure the following security parameters (make changes in the typical settings):

- Require a secured password

- Require data encryption (disconnect the connection if there is no encryption)

Note: Because the remote access server is not yet available, you will not be able to test the connection.

Steps

Complete the following steps:

1. Click **Start**. Right-click **My Network Places** and choose **Properties** from the menu.

2. In the left pane, click **Create a new connection** to open the Network Connection wizard.

3. Click **Next** to begin the wizard.

    Which option would you choose to connect your computer to another computer using a serial cable?

    _____

4. Select the **Connect to the network at my workplace** option and click **Next**.

5. Select the **Dial-up connection** option and click **Next**.

6. Type the name for the connection and click **Next**.

7. Type the phone number to dial and click **Next**.

8. Click **Finish** to create the connection.

9. To configure security for the connection, right-click the connection you created and select **Properties**.

10. Click the **Security** tab. The following dialog is shown.

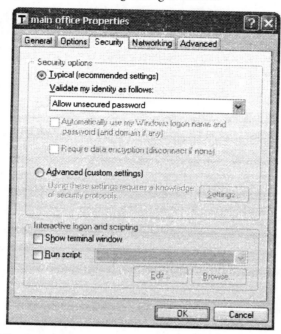

11. Configure the following options:

   ◦ In the **Validate my identity as follows** drop-down list, select **Require secured password**.

   ◦ Select **Require data encryption (disconnect if none)**.

   Click **OK**.

8.1.9 CONFIGURE ADVANCED AUTHENTICATION

Scenario

Your company provides dialup access to a remote access server so you can access company network resources while at home. You want to make sure that only secure authentication methods are used to connect to the remote access server.

Modify the existing dialup connection (called *Dial Company*). Edit the Advanced security settings for the connection as follows:

- Require encryption

- Use only MS-CHAP v2 authentication

Steps

Complete the following steps:

1. Click **Start**. Right-click **My Network Places** and choose **Properties** from the menu.

2. Right-click the connection you want to edit and select **Properties**.

3. Click the **Security** tab.

4. Click **Advanced (custom settings)**, then click the **Settings...** button. The following dialog is shown.

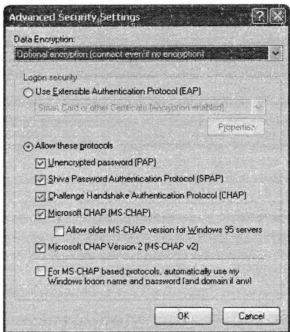

5. Configure the following settings:

    ◦   In the **Data Encryption** drop-down list, select **Require encryption (disconnect if server declines)**.

    ◦   Deselect all protocols except the **Microsoft CHAP Version 2 (MS-CHAP v2)** option.

    Click **OK**.

6. Click **OK**.

8.1.10 CONFIGURE SMART CARD FOR AUTHENTICATION

Scenario

Your company provides dialup access to a remote access server so you can access company network resources while at home. In an effort to secure the dialup connection, they have implemented a policy to require smart cards for all dialup connections.

Modify the existing dialup connection (called *Dial Company*) to use only smart cards for authentication. Edit the Advanced security settings for the connection as follows:

- Configure maximum strength encryption

- Enable EAP for authentication

- Select **Smart Card or other certificate** as the EAP type

Steps

Complete the following steps:

1. Click **Start**. Right-click **My Network Places** and choose **Properties** from the menu.

2. Right-click the connection you want to edit and select **Properties**.

3. Click the **Security** tab.

4. Click **Advanced (custom settings)**, then click the **Settings...** button.

5. Configure the following settings:

   ◦ In the **Data Encryption** drop-down list, select **Maximum strength encryption (disconnect if server declines)**.

   ◦ Select **Use Extensible Authentication Protocol (EAP)**.

   ◦ For the EAP type, select Smart Card or other Certificate (encryption enabled)

   Click **OK**.

6. Click **OK**.

8.2.4 CONFIGURE A VPN SERVER

Scenario

You want to let users connect to the Branch-Srv2 branch office's LAN via the Internet as shown in the following graphic.

Remote Access
Clients

Remote Access
Server

You decide to configure the Branch-Srv2 server as a Virtual Private Network (VPN) remote access server.

Your task in this lab is to:

- Configure the Branch-Srv2 server to accept VPN remote access connections.

- Select **Local Area Connection 2** as the Internet connection for the VPN server.

- Configure the server to route TCP/IP traffic from the Local Area Connection 2 network connection and to distribute IP addresses in the range 192.168.200.200 to 192.168.200.250 to remote access clients. RADIUS will not be used.

Note: The server has already been configured with certificates to support L2TP.

Steps

Use the Configure and Enable Routing and Remote Access wizard to configure the VPN server. When the wizard starts, select the **Remote Access (dial-up or VPN)** option.

Complete the following steps:

1. Click **Start/Administrative Tools/Routing and Remote Access** to open the Routing and Remote Access console.

2. Right-click the server and choose **Configure and Enable Routing and Remote Access** from the menu.

3. Click **Next** to start the Routing and Remote Access Server Setup wizard.

4. Select **Remote access (dial-up or VPN)** and click **Next**.

5. Check the **VPN** option and click **Next**.

6. Select **Local Area Connection 2** as the Internet connection. Click **Next**.

7. Select **From a specified range of addresses** and click **Next** to define the address range.

8. Click the **New...** button.

9. Type the beginning and ending IP addresses in the range. Click **OK**, then click **Next** to continue.

10. Verify that RADIUS is not used and click **Next**.

11. Click **Finish** to configure the router.

12. To verify the configuration, expand the server object and select **Ports**.

    How many L2TP and PPTP ports are defined?

8.2.5 DISABLE PPTP PORTS

Scenario

You have previously configured the Branch-Srv1 server for Virtual Private Network (VPN) remote access. However, you find that when clients connect, some connect using PPTP and others connect using L2TP. You want to force all connections to use L2TP or not to connect at all.

Your task in this lab is to:

•   Configure the Branch-Srv1 VPN server to use L2TP only for routing and remote access. In other words, disable all PPTP ports for routing and remote access.

•   Make 15 L2TP ports available for remote access.

Assume that all other configuration tasks have been completed.

Steps

Complete the following steps:

1.   Click **Start/Administrative Tools/Routing and Remote Access** to open the Routing and Remote Access console.

2.   Expand the server node and click the **Ports** container. Notice that there are both L2TP and PPTP VPN ports.

3. Right-click the **Ports** container and choose **Properties** from the menu. The following dialog is shown.

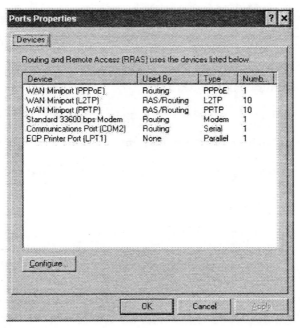

Notice the **Used By** column which indicates the services that the port is configured to use.

4. Select the **WAN Miniport (PPTP)** entry and click the **Configure...** button. The following dialog is shown.

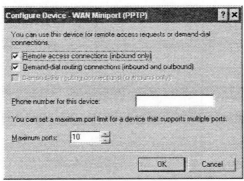

5. Set the **Maximum ports** box to **0**. Click **OK**.

   What happens?

   _____

6. Click **OK** to dismiss the message.

7. Change the **Maximum ports** value to **1**.

8. To disable PPTP on the router, deselect the following options:

   ○ **Remote access connections (inbound only)**

   ○ **Demand-dial routing connections (inbound and outbound)**

   Click **OK**.

   What might happen when you reduce the number of allowed ports?

   _____

9. Click **Yes**.

   How has the **Used By** column changed for the **WAN Miniport (PPTP)** entry?

   _____

10. Select the WAN Miniport (L2TP) entry and click the **Configure...** button.

11. Type the desired number of **Maximum ports**, then click **OK**.

12. Click **OK**. Verify that there are no PPTP ports and 15 L2TP ports listed in the console.

8.2.7 CREATE A CLIENT VPN CONNECTION

Scenario

You are configuring network connections for a portable Windows XP Professional computer. You want to let this computer connect to your company network remotely over a VPN connection.

Your task in this lab is to create a VPN connection that connects to your company's VPN remote access server. Configure the VPN connection with the following properties:

- Connection Name/Company Name = Company VPN

- Internet Connection to Automatically Use = Dial Internet

- VPN Server = 172.10.5.42

Steps

Complete the following steps:

1. Click **Start**. Right-click **My Network Places** and choose **Properties** from the menu.

2. In the left pane, click **Create a new connection** to open the Network Connection wizard.

3. Click **Next** to begin the wizard.

4. Select **Connect to the network at my workplace**. Click **Next**.

5. Select **Virtual Private Network connection**. Click **Next**.

6. Type the company name (this will become the name of the network connection). Click **Next**.

7. Verify that the dialup connection is select as the connection to use for the VPN. Click **Next**.

8. Type the host name or IP address of the VPN remote access server on the destination network. Click **Next**.

9. Click **Finish** to create the connection.

8.2.8 CUSTOMIZE THE TUNNELING PROTOCOL

Scenario

Your Windows XP Professional computer has a VPN connection called Company VPN. The connection uses the dialup connection to connect to the Internet and then establish the VPN connection. You want to make sure that the most secure form of VPN protocol is used for the connection.

Your task in this lab is to force the Company VPN connection to use L2TP with IPSec for the tunneling protocol.

Steps

Complete the following steps:

1. Click **Start**. Right-click **My Network Places** and choose **Properties** from the menu.

2. Right-click the VPN connection and select **Properties**.

3. Click the **Networking** tab. The following dialog is shown.

4. In the **Type of VPN server I am** calling drop-down list, select the type of VPN tunneling protocol you want to use.

5. Click **OK**.

9.0

Internet Services Security

9.1.4 CONFIGURE WEB SITE AUTHENTICATION

Scenario

Security has suddenly become a major concern for the Default Web Site. You no longer want anonymous access to the site to be permitted and want authentication to come from Active Directory domain accounts.

Your task in this lab is to:

- Disable anonymous access

- Enable Digest authentication

- Disable all other authentication methods

Steps

Enabling Digest authentication allows domain users to authenticate to the Web site using their domain account logon credentials.

Complete the following steps:

1. Click **Start/Administrative Tools/Internet Information Services (IIS) Manager**.

2. Expand the server object and the **Web Sites** node.

3. Right-click the **Default Web Site** and select **Properties**.

4. Click the **Directory Security** tab. The following dialog is shown.

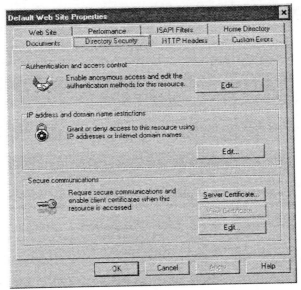

5. Click the **Edit...** button beneath **Authentication and access control**. The following dialog is shown.

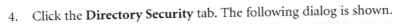

6. To force authentication to the Web site:

    ◦ Deselect **Enable anonymous access**

    ◦ Deselect **Integrated Windows authentication**

    ◦ Select **Digest authentication for Windows domain servers**

    What is the restriction with using Digest authentication?

    _____

7. Click **Yes**, then **OK**.

8. Click **OK** to close the Web site properties.

9.1.5 CONFIGURE WEB FOLDER AUTHENTICATION

Scenario

Your company intranet currently uses the Default Web Site for company-wide content. Because it is an intranet, anonymous authentication is allowed. The Web site includes a Security virtual directory that is used by the Human Resources department to store sensitive files. They want to secure access to those files by requiring authentication. However, you do not want to inconvenience all Web site users by requiring authentication for the entire Web site.

Your task in this lab is to require Windows Integrated authentication on the Security virtual directory.

Steps

Configure authentication for a virtual directory in a similar manner to configuring authentication for the Web site.

Complete the following steps:

1. Click **Start/Administrative Tools/Internet Information Services (IIS) Manager**.

2. Expand the server object, the **Web Sites** node, and the **Default Web Site** node.

3. Right-click the **Security** virtual directory and select **Properties**.

4. Click the **Directory Security** tab.

5. Click the **Edit...** button beneath **Authentication and access control**.

6. Make the following configuration changes:

   ○ Deselect **Enable anonymous access**

   ○ Select **Integrated Windows authentication**

   Click **OK**.

7. Click **OK** to close the virtual directory properties.

9.1.7 CONFIGURE IIS PERMISSIONS

Scenario

The Default Web Site on the Sea-IT-Srv1 server hosts the Web site for the company. A virtual directory called Data holds fact sheets for various company departments. You want to increase the security of the information in the Data virtual directory.

Your task in this lab is to change the permissions of the Data virtual directory as follows:

- Do not allow writing to the directory.

- Do not allow directory browsing.

- Do not allow scripts or executables to run.

Steps

Complete the following steps:

1. Click **Start/Administrative Tools/Internet Information Services (IIS) Manager**.

2. Expand the server object, the **Web Sites** node, and the **Default Web Site** node.

3. Right-click the **Data** virtual directory and select **Properties.** The following dialog is shown.

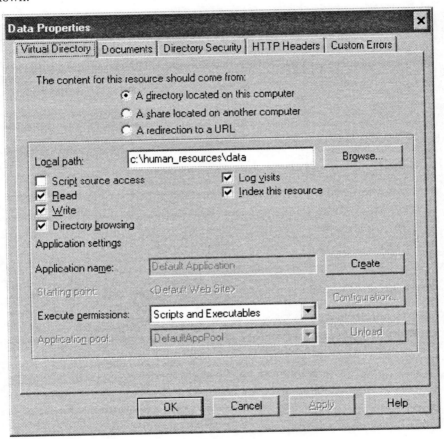

4. Make the following configuration changes:

   ○ Deselect **Write**

   ○ Deselect **Directory browsing**

   ○ For **Execute permissions**, specify **None**

   Click **OK**.

9.4.2 CLEAR THE BROWSER CACHE

Scenario

You are attending a conference. In the conference lobby are several computers with Internet access for use by attendees. You have just finished surfing the Internet and checking your e-mail. You want to make sure that information about the sites you visited, the passwords you typed, and any information you entered at Web sites is not stored on the local computer.

Your task in this lab is to clear the following items:

- Delete all cookies

- Delete all temporary Internet files, including offline files

- Clear the Web browser history

Note: On a live system, you can access the Internet Options through the **Tools/Internet Options...** menu of Internet Explorer. In this lab, go through the Control Panel to open Internet Options.

Steps

Complete the following steps:

1. Click **Start/Control Panel**.

2. Click **Switch to Classic View**.

3. Double-click **Internet Options**. The following dialog is shown.

4. Click the **Delete Cookies...** button. Click **OK**.

5. Click the **Delete Files...** button. Select **Delete all offline content** and click **OK**.

6. Click the **Clear History** button. Click **Yes**.

7. Click **OK**.

9.4.4 ADD A TRUSTED SITE

Scenario

You work for a biotech research firm and are trying to access a new internal Web server called acct.westsim.private. After logging on, you see a warning message that instructs you to add the site to your trusted site list.

Your task in this lab is to use Internet Options in the Control Panel to add the acct.westsim. private URL to the Trusted sites zone in Internet Explorer. The site does *not* support SSL (https). In the lab, precede the URL with either *http://* or *https://* as appropriate.

Steps

Complete the following steps:

1. Click **Start/Control Panel**.

2. Click **Switch to Classic View**.

3. Double-click **Internet Options**.

4. Click the **Security** tab. The following dialog is shown.

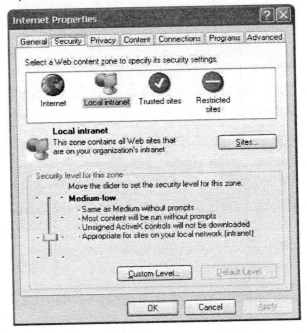

5.   Select the **Trusted Sites** zone, then click the **Sites...** button. The following dialog is shown.

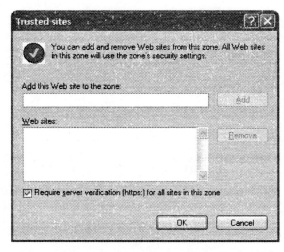

6.   Deselect the **Require server verification (https:) for all sites in this zone** option.

7.   Type the URL for the Web site. Use the following syntax for the URL: *http://acct.westsim. private.* Click **Add**.

8.   Click **OK**.

9.   Click **OK** to close the Internet Options.

9.4.5 ADD A RESTRICTED SITE

Scenario

You administer a Windows XP Professional computer. Users of the computer must often go to the www.networkinghistory.com Web site for reference information. However, they are inundated by popup advertisement screens when they surf that site. You discover that the popups for the site come from the following locations:

- http://www.myads.com

- http://www.badads.com

Disable popup ads by:

- Adding these two sites to the Restricted sites zone (be sure to precede each site with http://).

- Disabling Active scripting for the *Internet* zone (note that disabling this feature disables all scripts on the page).

Steps

Complete the following steps:

1. Click **Start/Control Panel**.

2. Click **Switch to Classic View**.

3. Double-click **Internet Options**.

4. Click the **Security** tab.

5. Select the **Restricted Sites** zone, then click the **Sites...** button.

6. Type the URL for the Web site. Use the following syntax for the URL: *http://www.myads. com*. Click **Add**. Repeat the process for any additional sites you want to add.

7.   Click **OK**.

Select each of the zones and note the default security level below.

Zone	Default Security Level
Internet	
Local intranet	
Trusted sites	
Restricted sites	

8.   Select the **Internet** zone, then click the **Custom Level...** button. The following dialog is shown.

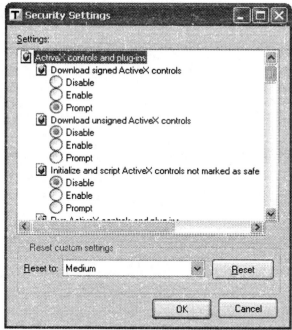

What is the default setting for the following options?

Option	Setting
Download signed ActiveX controls	
Download unsigned ActiveX controls	
File download	
Java permissions	
Launching programs and files in an IFRAME	

9. Locate the **Scripting/Active scripting** entry. Select **Disable**. Click **OK**.

What happened to the Internet zone security level?

_____

10. Click **OK** to close the Internet Options.

9.4.6 CUSTOMIZE ZONE SETTINGS

Scenario

You want to increase the security of Web browsing so that you have a better idea of what types of scripts and programs run through the browser. You want to configure certain settings so that you are unable to perform some tasks.

Your task in this lab is to edit the security for the Internet zone and configure the following settings:

- Run only Administrator approved Active X controls

- Disable Java

- Prevent submitting non-encrypted form data

Steps

Complete the following table with the necessary settings to meet the scenario requirements.

Option	Setting
ActiveX controls and plug-ins\Run ActiveX controls and plug-ins	
Microsoft VM\Java permissions	
Miscellaneous\Submit nonencrypted form data	

Complete the following steps:

1. Click **Start/Control Panel**.

2. Click **Switch to Classic View**.

3. Double-click **Internet Options**.

4. Click the **Security** tab.

5. Select the **Internet** zone, then click the **Custom Level...** button.

6. Configure the required security options. Click **OK**, then click **OK** again.

9.4.8 CHANGE THE COOKIE LEVEL

Scenario

You use a Windows XP computer at work. A recent security audit has recommended that you implement security for cookies stored on local computers. While you don't want to block cookies completely, you want to make sure that cookies can only be used on Web sites when you explicitly allow them.

Configure the privacy setting for your computer to the High default level.

Steps

Complete the following steps:

1. Click **Start/Control Panel**.

2. Click **Switch to Classic View**.

3. Double-click **Internet Options**.

4. Click the **Privacy** tab. The following dialog is shown.

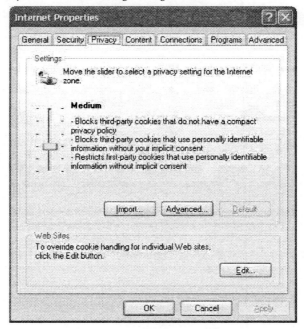

5. Move the slider to set the security level to **High.** Click **OK.**

9.4.9 CUSTOMIZE COOKIE HANDLING

Scenario

You work on a Windows XP Professional computer. You are concerned about your privacy when surfing the Web and would like to increase it. You want your computer to block cookies from banner ad companies such as Quadrupleclick.com, but you also want your computer to accept cookies from legitimate sites, such as your bank's Web site.

Edit the privacy settings in Internet Options to implement the following cookie settings:

- Always allow 1st party cookies

- Always block 3rd party cookies

- Accept session cookies

Steps

Complete the following steps:

1. Click **Start/Control Panel**.

2. Click **Switch to Classic View**.

3. Double-click **Internet Options**.

4. Click the **Privacy** tab.

5. Click the **Advanced...** button. The following dialog is shown.

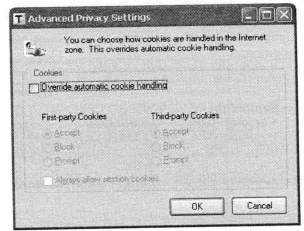

6. Select **Override automatic cookie handling** and configure the desired cookie settings. Click **OK**.

7. Click **OK**.

9.4.11 CONFIGURE BROWSER SECURITY

Scenario

You are a computer programmer for your company. You often download code modules from various sites on the Internet to use in your own projects. Recently, you have been asked by your manager to proactively increase the security of your Web surfing and downloading, so you decide to implement some advanced security measures in Internet Explorer.

Your tasks in this lab are to enable the following settings on your computer:

• Check for server certificate revocation

• Check for signatures on downloaded programs

Steps

Complete the following steps:

1. Click **Start/Control Panel**.

2. Click **Switch to Classic View**.

3. Double-click **Internet Options**.

4. Click the **Advanced** tab. The following dialog is shown.

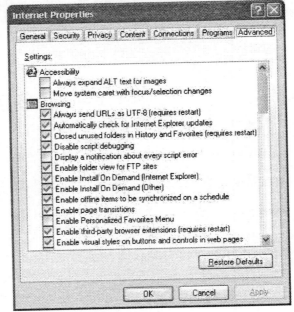

By default, which SSL levels are enabled?

_____

By default, what action will take place when an invalid site certificate is received?

_____

5. Enable or disable the features you want to customize.

6. Click **OK**.

9.4.12 CLEAR TEMPORARY INTERNET FILES

Scenario

Your company has a kiosk computer that is located in the lobby. Often, users on lunch drop by the kiosk to check e-mail through a Web site. You are concerned that a visitor might be able to use the kiosk and view information about the sites last visited, including the e-mail site.

Your task in this lab is to configure the computer to always delete files in the Temporary Internet Files folder when the browser is closed. Configure this setting on the Advanced tab of the Internet properties.

Steps

Complete the following steps:

1.   Click **Start/Control Panel**.

2.   Click **Switch to Classic View**.

3.   Double-click **Internet Options**.

4.   Click the **Advanced** tab.

5.   Below the Security heading, check the **Empty Temporary Internet Files folder when browser is closed** option.

6.   Click **OK**.